BOA
EDITIONS
LIMITED

The printing of this book was made possible, in part,
by a generous donation from
the Mary S. Mulligan Charitable Trust

You & Yours

Naomi Shihab Nye

AMERICAN POETS CONTINUUM SERIES, NO. 93

BOA EDITIONS, LTD. ROCHESTER, NY 2005

05 06 07 08 7 6 5 4 3 2

Publications by BOA Editions, Ltd. — a not-for-profit corporation under
section 501(c)(3) of the United States Internal Revenue Code — are made
possible with the assistance of grants from the Literature Program of the
New York State Council on the Arts; the Literature Program of the National
Endowment for the Arts; the Sonia Raiziss Giop Charitable Foundation; the
Lannan Foundation; the Mary S. Mulligan Charitable Trust; the County of
Monroe, NY; Rochester Area Community Foundation; the Elizabeth F.
Cheney Foundation; the Ames-Amzalak Memorial Trust in memory of
Henry Ames, Semon Amzalak and Dan Amzalak; the Chadwick-Loher
Foundation in honor of Charles Simic and Ray Gonzalez; the Steeple-Jack
Fund; the Chesonis Family Foundation, as well as contributions from many
individuals nationwide.

See Colophon on page 88 for special individual acknowledgments.
Cover Design: Geri McCormick
Cover Art: "Buzzload of Paranoia" by Charles Moody, courtesy of the artist
Interior Design and Composition: Scott McCarney
Manufacturing: McNaughton & Gunn, Lithographers

Library of Congress Cataloging-in-Publication Data

Nye, Naomi Shihab.
    You & yours : poems / by Naomi Shihab Nye.— 1st ed.
      p. cm. — (American poets continuum series; v. 93)
    ISBN 1-929918-69-0 (trade paper: alk. paper) —
    ISBN 1-929918-68-2 (tradecloth: alk. paper)
    I. Title. II. Series.
  PS3564.Y44Y68 2005
  811'.54—dc22   2005011360

BOA Editions, Ltd.
Thom Ward, Editor
David Oliveiri, Chair
A. Poulin, Jr., President & Founder (1938–1996)
260 East Avenue, Rochester, NY 14604
www.boaeditions.org

NATIONAL
ENDOWMENT
FOR THE ARTS

State of the Arts

NYSCA

With love for Michael, and for Madison, on his way.

And in memory of Daria Donnelly, the best friend poetry
(and many people) will ever know.

CONTENTS

TWO | YOURS

Cross that Line

Paul Robeson stood
on the northern border
of the USA
and sang into Canada
where a vast audience
sat on folding chairs
waiting to hear him.

He sang into Canada.
His voice left the USA
when his body was
not allowed to cross
that line.

Remind us again,
brave friend.
What countries may we
sing into?
What lines should we all
be crossing?
What songs travel toward us
from far away
to deepen our days?

ONE

You

Procrastination is the most creative act there is.

Those little test pots are the way I get started.
They're the best things I do.
Everything I do is test pots so now
there are no test pots.

—Rudolf Staffel, Noted Ceramic Artist

Family Land

The man on South Flores rearranging cedar branches
over the junk in his stolen shopping cart
the broken junk that is everything
the cart that holds everything
that lurches when he pushes
as if crossing an endless curb
is more proud than hungry
He will not accept food from anyone

The woman smoking
in front of the homeless shelter
on Soledad, *Lookit this picture*
of lungs my doctor gave me,
it looks worse than that burned
house we left

The man who steals bird baths, potted plants,
fern baskets from front yards and porches
thinks this is okay because his life
did not give him as much as other
peoples' lives gave them
If you met him at the Flea Market
and said *Hello? My bird bath?*
it would not register
would not register at all

Miss Pearl Augusta age 103
reads poetry from a giant book
on her coffee table
to stay fresh
the heat can't beat her back
she tops the thermometer one-on-one

Where is the spine of a summer?
Steam rising from shirts
Candida pins them up outside
before the clatter of cups
before the men who work on the roof down the street
arrive with hammers & chisels & tiles & glue
Clouds of dust all day, the drone of drilling
She prays the dust won't reach her line

Fold

I am partial to poems about
little ruinations, explosions of minor joy,
light falling on the heads of gentle elders.
Also the way pampas grasses look toward
the end of summer, shining, shaggy,
the quietude of their patient sway.
Cakes in a window do something for me too.
Even the doilies where cakes once sat
marked with small stains, crumbs of sugar . . .
can you see my proclivity for the words
"small" and "little," a diminutive tendency
in a world given often to the sprawling and huge?
You could try a pebble, a miniature box.
People with the patience for origami — well,
    I am not one,
but I like to see what they fold.
Toddlers in grocery carts
swinging plump legs make me pause –
how difficult not to touch them.
If you send something about a mound of lentils,
I will be intrigued. The general potency and power
of humankind, however, is hard for me to get my mind
around. Watch that girl guard her empty sack
after the muffin is gone, puffing it, listening to
its breath. Consider the blue velvet hair band
dropped in a puddle at the water park
or the small yellow shovel we found half-buried
    on the beach
at Kailua that we carried with us six months
    to every place
there were waves.

Someone I Love

Someone I love so much cut down my primrose patch. It looked like an oval of overgrown weeds to him, in the front yard, near the black mailbox on the post. He did not know that for weeks I had been carefully tending and watering it, as a few primroses floated their pink heads above the green mass, unfurled their delicate bonnets. With dozens of buds waiting to shine, we were on the brink, everything popping open, despite the headlines, all sweet flower beings from under the ground remembering what they were supposed to do.

He mowed it down with the old push lawn mower. I was out of town — he didn't ask his father, who knew how precious it was to me — his father was in the back while this was happening and didn't see — there wasn't a second thought — why would we have such a tall patch in the yard? — what does my mother do when she comes out here with the old shovel and the bucket and the mysterious sacks of rose food and mulch, poking around in the earth, trimming, the clippers in her pocket, bending to the wild tangle of jasmine on the fence, the Dutchman's Pipe, the happy oregano, the funny cacti crowding together in complicated profusion like a family, the miniature chiles — what does she do, why is this here?

He just cut it down. It wasn't easy.
He must have pushed really hard to get it to go.

When I stood outside in my nightie the next dreamy-sweet morning at dawn after returning home on the midnight plane, watering my bluebonnets snapdragons butterfly bush lantana, wanting to feel tied to earth again, as I always do when I get home, rooted in soil and stone and old caliche and bamboo and trees a hundred years of memory in their trunks and bushes we didn't plant, and the healthy *esperanza* never losing her hope, and the banana palms just poking out their fine and gracious greenery, when I suddenly saw what was gone, what wasn't there, not there, impossible, I was so shocked I let the hose run all over my bare feet. The cold stun of fury filled me, sorrow rising and pouring into questions, who could do this, why, how could anyone? I thought of the time my daddy came home to find every head cut off his giant sunflowers right after they had opened their faces to the sky, only the empty stalks remaining, his disbelieving sorrow as he went to his room and lay down on the bed and closed his eyes, and thought, I will not mention this, I am too sad to mention it, this is the pain of people everywhere, the pain this year deserves.

But at breakfast I went a little strange like the lady down the street who shows up at people's doors with a snarling dog and a hammer in her pocket, I went wild and furious and he swore they just looked like weeds to him, why hadn't I warned him, why did I only tell Dad?

I pointed them out to you weeks ago, I said.
He said, I don't remember flower things like that.

And it was the season of blooming and understanding. It was the season of hiding from headlines, wondering what it would do if the whole house had been erased or just the books and paintings or what about the whole reckless garden or (then it gets unthinkable but we make ourselves think it now and then to stay human) the child's arms or legs, what would I do? If I did not love him, who would I become?

Sewing, Knitting, Crocheting

(Mother's Day 1999)

A small striped sleeve in her lap,
navy and white,
needles carefully whipping in yarn
from two sides.
She reminds me of the wide-angled women
filled with calm
I pretended to be related to
in crowds.

In the next seat
a yellow burst of wool
grows into a hat with a tassel.
This woman looks young to crochet.
I'm glad history isn't totally lost.
Her silver hook dips gracefully.

And when's the last time you saw
anyone sew a pocket onto a gray linen shirt
in public?
Her stitches must be invisible.
A bevelled thimble glitters in the light.

On Mother's Day
three women who aren't together
conduct delicate operations
in adjoining seats
between La Guardia and Dallas.
Miraculously, they never speak.
Three different kinds of needles,
three snippy scissors (in the old days,
when you could carry scissors and knives),

everyone else on the plane
snoozing with *The Times*.
When the flight attendant
offers free wine to celebrate,
you'd think they'd sit back,
chat a minute,
trade patterns, yes?

But a grave separateness
has invaded the world.
They sip with eyes shut
and never say
Amazing
or
Look at us
or
May your thread
never break.

Last August Hours Before the Year 2000

Spun silk of mercy,
long-limbed afternoon,
sun urging purple blossoms from baked stems.
What better blessing than to move without hurry
under trees?
Lugging a bucket to the rose that became a twining
house by now, roof and walls of vine —
you could live inside this rose.
Pouring a slow stream around the
ancient pineapple crowned with spiky fruit,
I thought we would feel old
by the year 2000.
Walt Disney thought cars would fly.

What a drama to keep thinking *the last summer*
the last birthday
before the calendar turns to zeroes.
My neighbor says anything we plant
in September takes hold.
She's lining pots of little grasses by her walk.

I want to know the root goes deep
on all that came before,
you could lay a soaker hose across
your whole life and know
there was something
under layers of packed summer earth
and dry blown grass
to moisten.

Frequent Frequent Flyer

I realized that I travel too much on the day I began tidying an airport as if it were my bedroom. Unconsciously I picked up subscription cards that had slipped from magazines, loose newspaper sections, empty soda cups, and pitched them into the trash. Hey, it was *my gate*. I wanted it to look nice. The prim decisiveness of airports feels deeply pleasing and restful. The anonymity, a gust of fresh air. Neat signage, changing gate information, moving sidewalks, minimalist trains "arriving in 2 minutes" — delicious. Why do so many people complain about airports? How hard is it to show one's ID? A few weeks ago, I was at La Guardia long enough to start a small business. I know Houston's Hobby and Washington's Reagan as well as the blocks around our house. I love Chicago's neon tunnel and the Tom's Toothpaste display in Portland, Maine. Portland's airport, however, does not sell Tom's Toothpaste. In San Antonio we display Mexican tile sinks. You could rally some Tom's Toothpaste and brush your teeth over them. I like putting things together, imagining lives. Where are all these people *going?* So many children traveling alone . . . I know which stalls nationwide serve the best sesame bagel, the tastiest swirled vanilla and chocolate frozen yogurt. The Cincinnati chili stand has added vegetarian chili to its spaghetti/chili/cheese list. I am such a frequent flyer, I could become a flight attendant tomorrow with no training. Perhaps this is insulting to the profession, surely attendants do many crucial things we never see, but I find myself mouthing their safety instructions perfectly and sometimes, after serving drinks at my own home, I walk around with a trash bag and a grim smile. It is true that on all sides at every gate, frantic women and men are punching numbers into little phones. Soon they will be condemned to live two whole hours without calling anyone . . . this is hard for them. It makes no difference whether I am headed to Seattle, Winnipeg, Toronto, Boise — airport is the hopeful second home place, the precious *enroute*, the hour you could be anyone who ever passed through.

Stay

1

When Angus Campbell, driver of the Bowman's Coach
on the Isle of Mull points out his own white cottage
perched against a shimmering *loch*, he says,
"That's where I *stay*," not *live* and I remember
my friend back in Texas mentioning
that's what kids in rough neighborhoods say.
All day the word holds itself inside me,
a small net. We stay alert, gazing across waters,
casting ourselves toward ancient altars,
a young woman selling calendula cream
by a dock, *heals anything* —
may we stay longer than the ferry please?
Stay through the winter?
Till a sheen of gray rain absorbs this pliable light?
Angus points out the Tragedy Cottage where
centuries ago, a tumbling boulder
crushed a bride & groom on their first night.
It sits, still, inside the perimeter of the ruined home.
Had they lived long lives,
we might not think of them now.
So brief, such a swift surge of joy,
I close my eyes to see the fearless puffins
on the Isle of Staffa, darting across mossy cliffs,
welcoming people who have never in their memory
hurt them. *Stay, for everything tender,*
teacups lined neatly on a side table,
crystal salt cellars with wee silver spoons,
melodious Scottish voices stitching the seam
of late and early light,
the night the sun dotted its own "i" in the sea —
and, I swear it, rabbits at dawn in a circle

on the lawn, I saw with my own eyes
from the turret window —
say, would you mind terribly going on without me?

2

Sheep on a moor keep to their task,
clumped in threes or widely spaced.
Their days appear to open and close
in the same dull way, but what do we know?
We raced each other to breakfast
in our castle lodging more than once.

Surprise sheep on a road and they startle,
currents flowing two directions –
they do not crave our company.
Fields dotted with thick white wool
from plush coats,
softness among stones.

3

Tell me the ocean is small.
Time holds us in its pocket
and another year's jingle might find us here again,
staring from the same turret window —
green swoops, layerings of moor — what's said already —
against the streaked north Atlantic that keeps
rewriting itself, and the eloquent silence,
blue, or frocked, or misted,
the well that won't go dry
and won't write itself down either,
not in any keeping way — the unspoken still-to-be
taking its own slow time behind all of ours.

Isle of Mull, Scotland

Because by now we know everything is not so green
    elsewhere.

The cities tied their nooses around our necks,
we let them without even seeing.

Not even feeling our breath soften
as clumps of shed wool scattered across days.

Not even. This even-ing, balance beam of light on green,
the widely lifted land, resonance of moor
winding down to water, the full of it. Days of cows
and sheep bending their heads.

We walked where the ancient pier juts into the sea.
Stood on the rim of the pool, by the circle
of black boulders. No one saw we were there
and everyone who had ever been there
stood silently in air.

Where else do we ever have to go, and why?

Pimento

Tell them Mr. Tennessee Williams has signed his last autograph, he said, sighing richly, lolling back in an overstuffed chair, asking for olives. Did I look like a bodyguard? A maid? At age 24, thunderstruck by proximities, I would stand between him and his readers. Against the luscious green brocade, he flexed his shoulders, closed his eyes. Balanced a green olive with a dash of red on his lower lip, popped it in. A woman with a book dashed forward. *Mr. Tennessee Williams has signed his last autograph*, I said, raising my elbow. She looked horrified. Her friends lifted dainty glasses of wine near a lamp with a stained shade. William Stafford held a paper plate carefully, tiny diamonds of crackers and cheese. He liked them. He would sign anything. And here was Ken Kesey wearing a fuzzy orange poncho, saying I would be a better singer if I sang more like Bob Dylan. Well, who wouldn't be? William Burroughs urged me to up my intake of Vitamin C.

Don Chu Go

Don chu go talkin bout the sunrise
purty pinky sunrise
as if they ain't all kinda people
suffrin evry corner a this world.

Remember them you hear?
I don wan no purty dove
sittin on a cedar poem
till all yer ancestors an mine
are walkin free. We got work to do.
Hear me?
No sirree girl don chu go
hangin up this phone!

I know yer type.
You think it's okay
ta cuddle yer sorrow
hide behinda bush
lookit little stones
lemme find a shiny one!
Cracks ina ground
like they got some kinda wisdom
well i do think they know morin
most of us but that
aint no way to spend a day.
Use yer voice!
Cry out fer pain, injustice,
come on lazy girl
don't be satisfied with dillydallydaisy poems
you don pay nuf attention to rough stuff.
People are dyin! I want you to shout!

Thats what the owl an I talked about this morning
in Brackenridge Park.

Now I'm gonna get off
let you go about yer business
but goddam it better be real business
or you gonna hear it
from yer ol buddy.

                                        (in memory, Maury Maverick Jr.)

Correspondence

Even Antonio Machado's house was closed for repairs.
Reporting on a journey,
my friend writes "robbed" and "rain"
and "disappointments." The pilgrimage
cancelled. Planes late.
Now it's time for
work again and this year
so many hopeful students
crowding his door
but he wishes he had more time
to prepare for them or better stories
to butter the path. Why is summer so
fast?

Last year we thought this year
would be better and this year last year
looks pretty good.
Sorry to be so glum,
I just wanted to know what
Antonio Machado might have kept
on his writing desk.

Headache

So we're sitting in Montreal in a pizza kitchen telling what
we carry in our memory sacks and Claire (wearing a coat
with a broken zipper, like childhood) remembers getting me
to ask our second-grade teacher back in St. Louis how to
spell "headache" 45 years ago. *Huh?* "Because I wanted to
write her a note," Claire says, grinning. "An *anonymous*
note saying, "Your loud voice gives me a headache," but
didn't know how to spell it. So I begged you to go find out.
You know how she always told us to use the dictionary? For
some reason, that time she didn't mention the dictionary to
you. Maybe you looked weird or something. She spelled it
and you copied the word, came back to your seat and
handed it to me under the table. I wrote in large script,
"Your voice gives me a headache," folded the note neatly,
and deposited it secretly at her place when we filed out for
recess. When we returned from the playground, I saw her
unfold it." Claire stares at me expectantly. "Then what?" I
say. "Did I get in trouble? Were you setting me up? Did she
think I wrote it?" How naïve was I, exactly? Claire had the
best handwriting in our class, this I distinctly recall. All
these years later she still has thick blonde hair and a
penchant for the wacky. "She burst into giggles and put her
head down on her desk because she couldn't stop laughing,"
Claire says triumphantly. "Yes, it's true. And she spoke
softly all afternoon."

Please Describe How You Became a Writer

Possibly I began writing as a refuge from our insulting first grade text book. *Come, Jane, come. Look, Dick, look.* Were there ever duller people in the world? You had to tell them to look at things? Why weren't they looking to begin with?

Bucket

Your eyes stayed closed for days and days
after you were born.
You did not want to eat or see us.
So much work was coming,
mountains to learn.

That year we had rain
every day in June. Cars washed
into gullies. I felt lonesome without *bond w/ her baby*
you in my body anymore.

Someone said, *take a walk around the block*
without the baby. Two blocks. Take a break.
A raggedy man drowned in the swollen
river behind our house, leaving a
fish in a bucket. What were we all
doing wrong?

Dialing the nurses at the hospital, I said *community*
I missed them. They told me how to hold you *est w/ the*
when you were deep *nurses.*
in that wordless world,
to wait until you were hungry.
Do you miss that world?
Some days it rained six inches.

Clearing

Last year our son gave me
a fat pink eraser for Christmas.
I never used it,
it's still sitting on my desk.

This year he handed over
fifteen plump pink erasers
encased in plastic
sealed with a snap.
And didn't laugh.
It's been harder and harder
having a bossy mom around.

O yes I remember
walking down by the drainage ditch
when I was a teen,
needing to erase something,
my parents' arguing and blame,
the way they knew me
better than I did,
or so they said,
knew which friends
were bad for me,
because they loved me,
of course they loved me.

With a single word — *Enough!*
or — *Okay!* — I would rise
and step outside
into a pink sky that
softened painlessly into
radiant stripes.

And I would walk under it,
and own it,
past the small sad houses,
down the hill lined with trees,
away from my family.
Feeling closer to birds
than any person,

longing for another nest,
clearing the language that fed me
clean from my mind,
but just for a time.
Just for a short time.

Tell Me About Yourself When You Were 17

We would lie down on the grass in the steamy dark, cypress trees rimming our kisses, their stoic, silent height. Was it bad luck to kiss on a grave? No one could have told us how much would disappear within a year. The best cat, run over by the one who loved him. Grandmother, and the lady who owned the horses. My favorite field. I would stroke your smooth Mexican skin and you would not talk to me, hardly ever, but you would meet me on the plot of the 1924 priest and close your eyes. I could feel the cloud passing over the moon even without looking up and I would never find you in a telephone book for the rest of my life.

Birthday

A single day illuminating him among women & men
this tender day with no mother in it for so many years

Once she bent over a table
setting out silver forks for the party

the same table he was not allowed to crawl under
blowing out candles was also frowned upon

so many things frowned upon
in the early days that shaped us

surrounded now by friends who love him
rich talk sharp cheese

somehow we have made
something of our lives

the years we never thought would stick to us have stuck
now we are as old as people in the stories

people in the forests
stirring moss into their soups

First Day Without You in 99 Years

Postman climbs onto creaky porch.
Not right, not right.
He didn't get the news.
Bitter leaf, bottom of cup.
No one laps it up.
Salty edge.
Where will the white coverlet migrate?
Staring at branches above curtains
day after day,
you waited to feel better,
you willed the leaves back
from their sleep.
Now what will we do?

Guide

My neighbor knew the exact location
of every map   every postcard & pincushion
       every empty basket
that once held chocolate eggs

In her tall house
       a century of spunk & clutter
       Please get me   she would say
guiding from her wheelchair
       in the other room
no, a little to the left of
       the nail clippers
there, that's it,
       in the orange tin
yes, you have it!

a folded essay about artifacts or water conservation
a purple ribbon or a pill that cost 3 dollars
she hated the pill that cost 3 dollars
when her father owned the 6th car
       in the state of Texas
& ran a drugstore
       no pill cost 3 dollars

I tried to memorize charms & Mexican pottery
       dolls & laces crowding the dresser,
          exactly the ways they stood
through wars & revolutions
       calmly   calmly
a glass case of miniature teacups
even clumps of dust on the ceiling
       over the bed

so that after her sudden terrible departure
as the icons were lifted & boxed & bagged
        for the highest bidders
                her voice from the other room
kept describing   what we'd find

Renovation

It cheered me that the man and woman ripping our house apart were a married couple. Maybe this meant they would be more careful with things. Delia neatly packed all the belongings from the rooms where mold was detected in large cardboard boxes marked KITCHEN ITEAMS and BATH — the mugs, spatulas, pots and pans, towels, bottles of shampoo. Chico draped large sheets of plastic from the 13-foot high ceilings for "containment." Then they both donned plastic space suits and face masks and began smashing the hundred year old green and white tile of the kitchen counter and the blue Mexican bird tile in the bathroom to take it out. The mold was under wood and sheetrock. It likes to eat adhesive. A very subversive guest. Goodbye familiar cracks and rounded edges. Goodbye heavy wooden drawers and stained porcelain bathtub. Our neighbors looked scared when they saw the spacemen in the yard. We moved out for five weeks

Mold is not a very glamorous topic, but it could be growing inside anybody's walls at any moment, finding its own safe harbor of moist secrecy, spreading and thickening in green or black creepy glory. You could have it too. We had mostly green but a little black. It gave me asthma even before it started sneaking out of a hole in the ceiling over the bathtub. Thanks to a leak in the roof and two other unrelated leaks in two wall-pipes we had it. Our hundred-year-old cottage was sabotaged. But considering all the possibilities for leakage in this world, it amazes me that more things don't leak. It amazes me that poop goes into the poop pipe and relatively clean water comes out of the faucet. It all amazes me. I know some people who have had to bulldoze their entire houses and throw away all their belongings thanks to mold. Delia called me into the front yard to see the boards from our bathroom wrapped in plastic. She pointed. There, there it is. See those little black and green spots? It is going away now. We are hauling it to the DUMP. You won't have it any more.

So we moved back into our house without any running water or toilets, it was like camping out at home. We ate peaches and icy cherry tomatoes from a big bowl. We drank coffee and made rum drinks in the afternoons, trying to replicate the happy hour at the hotel down the street, but it did not feel as fun. We drove around in the summer heat through traffic to gaze at tile and bathroom fixtures in too many stores and talked to carpenters and lighting experts and tried to make decisions. There are some people in the world who are good at doing this. We are not among them.

And then we waited. For someone to come measure. For substances to arrive from different directions. For things not to be broken. For them to be re-ordered. For someone to be able to put them in. Renovation involves mostly waiting. For the electrician who knows you cannot deal with those wires yourself. For the evangelical electrician's helper who says we will soon all be washing dishes in our yards. He does not like to go under the house. For the carpenter who looks uncannily like my gynecologist. For the diverter switch to arrive at a plumbing warehouse. For windows. For the counter installers who asked, how do you make a rose bush have more roses? What does it want and need? We started receiving mysterious catalogues like "Rest Room World."

During all this, the Palestinians overseas were being confined to their homes, if they had homes, or to their shacks, rooms, tents, and hovels. They could not go out to buy fresh oranges. They could not go to school. More houses were being seized and demolished daily. The word "demolished" sounds softer than it is. But in the documentary movie "Gaza Strip" you can hear the terrifying crashing sounds of giant bulldozers as they knock down houses a hundred years old. One gets tired of saying or hearing the words but it keeps happening. The whole time we were putting our house back together, more Palestinians were losing their homes. Suicide bombers, those tragic people driven insane by oppression, do not come out of vacuums. They come out of demolished homes. They saw their fathers blindfolded, hauled off to prison in buses. They saw their friends gassed by poison, blown up, intestines strewn in the dust. Their mothers wailing and bloody. Why is this almost never considered in the news? Sometimes where everything comes from is just as critical as where everything is going.

I hate this, said the teenager we live with, one rare night when I asked him to help me wash and rinse dishes in a pan in the yard. We had had company for dinner. It was fun to have company with no running water or bathroom. They were a little taken aback. I poured water over their hands from a pitcher. They tried not to look at all the boxes piled up in the dining room. The teenager scraping plates said, how long is this going to go on? Don't some people get their whole houses rebuilt in, like, a week? Why is it taking so long for this to be completed?

Just think, I said to him. (This is never a good idea to say to a teen person, but I said it anyway.) Just consider someone coming and taking our house away, while we're in the middle of fixing things, while everything is a mess. How would you feel? They would say your room is their room. Your computer is now their computer. Or they would blow up your room and say, Ah, too bad, we call it security, no one cares if you suffer.

What are you talking about? he said. I'd call the police!

What if you had no phone lines? What if the police had no power?

Stop talking like this. The mosquitoes are killing me. I hate washing dishes.

Our Time

Robert Frost wrote "Stopping by Woods on a Snowy Evening"
in the middle of a searing hot July.

Maybe he needed a chill, the silence
of frozen trees, to keep the air moving

in his mind. So many readers have considered
his two roads of another poem,

but maybe sweating Mr. Frost invoking frost,
his secret quirky inversion, matters more.

We grew up proud of our country.
Forests of wonderful words to wander through —

freedom, indivisible.
Now my horse is lost in a sheen of lies.

The world is lovely, dark, and deep.
We honor others as they sleep.

As they wake and as they sleep.

Fresh

To move
cleanly.
Needing to be
nowhere else.
Wanting nothing
from any store.
To lift something
you already had
and set it down in
a new place.
Awakened eye
seeing freshly.
What does that do to
the old blood moving through
its channels?

Lives of the Women Poets

(from biographical notes in
The Things That Matter edited by Julia Neuberger)

Essentially she is not very well-remembered.
She had a happy but limited childhood.
After she married the easy-going Tommy Tucker,
also known as "the Skipper" her years were rich
in love and devotion but short on cash and comfort.
Most of her work went and goes unread.
It deserves at least a second look.
She *was* T.S. Eliot's secretary.
Most of her poetry is hard reading these days.
Now and then we are grateful for a sense of humor popping up.
She never enjoyed good health.
Her most famous love conquest was George Bernard Shaw.
Her poetry has been subject to a lot of criticism.
Her content is not always to today's taste.
Her work ought to appear immature, which it does not.
No longer able to play the violin, she took to writing poetry.
Her husband was smitten with acute neuritis.
She was, despite everything, an extraordinary woman.
Her poetry was not what made her memorable.
She expressed well the turbulent passions of her soul,
but never attained her sister's success or popularity.
After her death, her sister would not allow
anything of Jewish interest to be included
in her collected works.
Her life was secluded, isolated, but her death was brave.
She did not relish the idea of a prolonged death.
Her poetry is most fascinating when it is not clear
to whom it is addressed.

Canoeing with Alligators

They won' make any bother.
Jes' paddle down center o' the stream.
They won' jump into yo' boat.
They only bother if you had a dog wit' you or somethin'.
Sho, they'd like to eat the dog.
People who wen' out canoe right befo' you took a dog.
No I didn' tell them that.
They didn' ask.
Brain a' alligator size o' green pea.
Private parts inside de body.
Can't tell outside, girl or boy —
even if ya turned one over, couldn't tell.
And didya know? Alligator born with a egg tooth.
They hatch theyself. Born knowin' how to hunt.
Have to — mama doesn't provide for 'em.
Sho, she sit on the eggs, protect 'em till they hatch,
    but thass it.
Once they born, nuthin' more to do wit' em.
Year later, if baby swim back in mama' pass,
    she might eat 'im.
Eat her own young.
But you got nuttin' to worry about.
She don' know you.
Jes' don' go lookin' pale like a marshmallow.
They see pale real good.
Alligator got no taste buds. Ain't choosy.
Don' put your hand over de edge of de boat
and don' feed 'em, definitely don' feed 'em.
Like dose dad-gum swamp tours feedin' 'em
all kinda chicken meat an' stuff, don' do it.
Like dose kids right over on de bank dere,
dey should know betta'. Dey live heah.

Only one time lately alligator jump into somebody canoe.
When two canoe pass an' he got caught in de middle.
Jes' tryin' to escape.
But that won't happen to you.

TWO

Yours

"... What you fear
will not go away; it will take you into
yourself and bless you and keep you.
That's the world, and we all live there."

— William Stafford
from *"For My Young Friends Who Are Afraid"*

Dictionary in the Dark

A retired general said
"the beautiful thing about it"
discussing war.
We were making "progress"
in our war effort.
"The appropriate time to launch the bombers"
pierced the A section with artillery as
"awe" huddled in a corner
clutching its small chest.
Someone else repeated, "in harm's way,"
strangely popular lately,
and "weapons of mass destruction"
felt gravely confused about their identity.
"Friendly" gasped. Fierce and terminal.
It had never agreed to sit beside fire, never.

�֍

The Day

I missed the day
on which it was said
others should not have
certain weapons, but we could.
Not only could, but should,
      and do.
I missed that day.
Was I sleeping?
I might have been digging
in the yard,
doing something small and slow
as usual.
Or maybe I wasn't born yet.
What about all the other people
who aren't born?
Who will tell them?

Your Weight, at Birth

Watching the Palestinian men
emerge from the Church of the Nativity,
I considered birth: being born into light again
after so many cramped weeks inside,
born into air & space,
how we wish the best for one another when someone
is being born, born into deportation & exile,
born, & banished.

Across the street, their women were wailing.
They could not greet or hug them.
The men were shuffled onto buses
to be sent away.
On the white & dusty street of Bethlehem,
where so many travelers have stood
holding candles, wrapped in song,
the prisoner men, in their own town.

An American TV announcer's voice sounded excited
to be present at the births —
over & over again
he hailed the table of sandwiches & bottled water
provided by Israeli soldiers
who actually looked perplexed
whenever the camera came in close.

One is born to wear a helmet, carry large artillery.
One is born to be thin, to wear raggedy clothes
& be shot in the leg. And some are born
to wonder, wonder, wonder.

For Mohammed Zeid of Gaza, Age 15

There is no _stray_ bullet, sirs.
No bullet like a worried cat
crouching under a bush,
no half-hairless puppy bullet
dodging midnight streets.
The bullet could not be a pecan
plunking the tin roof,
not hardly, no fluff of pollen
on October's breath,
no humble pebble at our feet.

So don't gentle it, please.

We live among stray thoughts,
tasks abandoned midstream.
Our fickle hearts are fat
with stray devotions, we feel at home
among bits and pieces,
all the wandering ways of words.

But this bullet had no innocence, did not
wish anyone well, you can't tell us otherwise
by naming it mildly, this bullet was never the friend
of life, should not be granted immunity
by soft saying — friendly fire, straying death-eye,
why have we given the wrong weight to what we do?

Mohammed, Mohammed, deserves the truth.
This bullet had no secret happy hopes,
it was not singing to itself with eyes closed —
under the bridge.

❈

54

Handwritten annotations:

- ADRESSING SOME SORT OF OFFICAL MOST LIKELY SOLDIERS.
- SMILIE COMPARING A STRAY BULLET TO A WORRIED CAT. IMAGE OF CAT CROUCHING WORRIED UNDER A BUSH.
- IMAGE,
- LOUD, MASSIVE IMPACTS / NOTHING PEACEFUL / — MISREPRESENTATION
- SO DON'T MAKE IT SOMETHING ITS NOT, IT'S NOT GENTLE, IT'S DEVISTATING DON'T SYMPATHIZE FOR SOLDIERS
- HUMAN NATURE →
- REPITION OF "STRAY" CENTRAL THEME OF POEM, STRAY BULLETS, STRAY THOUGHTS.
- REPITION OF STRAY AGAIN WORDS CAN BE DRIVING
- REINFORCEMENT
- ILL INTENT → PERSONIFICA...
- PARTICULAR BULLET
- CONVINCED
- AUTHOR HAS STRONG NEGATIVE FEELING TOWARD BULLET.
- YOUNG BOY
- AUTHOR IS ENGLOGING? THAT THEY ARE SENIORS THEMSELVES.
- QUESTION — WE ARE FICKLE, DON'T TAKE ACTION PURPOSING WE DO?
- ambiguous lang.
- PERSONIFIES Mohammed
- picture of boy contrary to media portrayal

The Story, Around the Corner

is not turning the way you thought
it would turn, gently, in a little spiral loop,
the way a child draws the tail of a pig.
What came out of your mouth,
a riff of common talk.
As a sudden weather shift on a beach,
sky looming mountains of cloud
in a way you cannot predict
or guide, the story shuffles elements, darkens,
takes its own side. And it is strange.
Far more complicated than a few phrases
pieced together around a kitchen table
on a July morning in Dallas, say,
a city you don't live in, where people
might shop forever or throw a thousand stories
away. You who carried or told a tiny bit of it
aren't sure. Is this what we wanted?
Stories wandering out,
having their own free lives?
Maybe they are planning something bad.
A scrap or cell of talk you barely remember
is growing into a weird body with many demands.
One day soon it will stumble up the walk and knock,
knock hard, and you will have to answer the door.

During a War

Best wishes to you & yours,
he closes the letter.

For a moment I can't
fold it up again —
where does "yours" end?
Dark eyes pleading
what could we have done
differently?
Your family,
your community,
circle of earth, we did not want,
we tried to stop,
we were not heard
by dark eyes who are dying
now. How easily they
would have welcomed us in
for coffee, serving it
in a simple room
with a radiant rug.
Your friends & mine.

The Sweet Arab, the Generous Arab

Since no one else is mentioning you enough.

The Arab who extends his hand. — OUT OF RESPECT, CURTOSEY
The Arab who will not let you pass
his tiny shop without a welcoming word.
The refugee inviting us in for a Coke.
Clean glasses on a table in a ramshackle hut.
Those who don't drink Coke would drink it now.
We drink from the silver flask of hospitality.
We drink and you bow your head.

Please forgive everyone who has not honored your name.

You who would not kill a mouse, a bird.
Who feels sad sometimes even cracking an egg.
Who places two stones on top of one another
for a monument. Who packed the pieces,
carried them to a new corner. For whom the words
rubble and blast are constants. Who never wanted
those words. To be able to say,
this is a day and I live in it safely,
with those I love, was all. Who has been hurt
but never hurt in return. Fathers and grandmothers,
uncles, the little lost cousin who wanted only
to see a Ferris wheel in his lifetime, ride it
high into the air. And all the gaping days
they bought no tickets
for spinning them around.

Why I Could Not Accept Your Invitation

Besides the fact that your event
is coming up in three weeks
on the other side of the world
and you just invited me *now*,
your fax contained the following phrases:
action-research oriented initiative;
regionally based evaluation vehicles;
culture should impregnate all different sectors;
consumption of cultural products;
key flashpoints in thematic areas.
Don't get me wrong, I love what you are doing,
believing in art and culture,
there, in the country next to the country
my country has recently been devastating
in the name of democracy,
but that is not the language I live in
and so I cannot come.
I live in teaspoon, bucket, river, pain,
turtle sunning on a brick.
Forgive me. Culture is everything
right about now. But I cannot pretend
a scrap of investment in the language
that allows human beings to kill one another
systematically, abstractly, distantly.
The language wrapped around 37,000,
or whatever the number today,
dead and beautiful bodies thrown into holes
without any tiny, reasonable *goodbye*.

❖

He Said EYE-RACK

Relative to our plans for your country,
we will blast your tree, crush your cart,
stun your grocery.
Amen sisters and brothers,
give us your sesame legs,
your satchels, your skies.
Freedom will feel good
to you too. Please acknowledge
our higher purpose. No, we did not see
your bed of parsley. On St. Patrick's Day
2003, President Bush wore a blue tie. Blinking hard,
he said, "We are not dealing with peaceful men."
He said, "reckless aggression."
He said, "the danger is clear."
Your patio was not visible in his frame.
Your comforter stuffed with wool
from a sheep you knew. He said, "We are
against the lawless men who
rule your country, not you." Tell that
to the mother, the sister, the bride,
the proud boy, the peanut-seller,
the librarian careful with her shelves.
The teacher, the spinner, the sweeper,
the invisible village, the thousands of people
with laundry and bread, the ants tunneling
through the dirt.

The Wreath that Eats Two Ice Cubes

A live green wreath featuring tiny red berries
sits in a damp glass pie plate on our table.

Each day I feed it two ice cubes
following instructions from its box.
I mist the delicate leaves.

The wreath will stay alive all winter
on this diet.

The wreath waits to make people feel festive,
to have us gather round it with plates & glasses
& shining spoons.
The wreath doesn't want us to watch the news.

Peace Pilgrim, You Are Still Walking

on the long roads, late at night. So many years
after you died, you're not off the hook, you're keeping
the pace, swinging your strong arms.
Who among us found a clearer way?
I shall not accept more than I need
while others in the world have less than they need.
We can work on inner peace and world peace
at the same time. Little people of the world,
may we never feel helpless again.
I marveled at your many-layered pinecone heart
and 3 possessions: toothbrush, postage stamps, comb.
Walk till given shelter, fast till given food.
Still, you're starting before dawn,
pausing at a roped-off trail that says,
THIS IS NO LONGER A FOOTPATH,
shaking your head. I'm sorry you can't rest yet.
One day I woke thinking, it's good you're dead.
We're still fools in a world of war.
Then I recalled the navy canvas of your suit,
how it always felt fresh, not tired.
We listened as hard as we could. What can't we learn?
I would establish a peace department in our government.
Under the swollen orange moon.
On the rim of the sad city, in a cardboard box under the
    overpass,
you held the calm and the strong conviction.
Oh Peace. Dear Peace.
Don't give up on us. Don't leave us stranded, please.

The Boy Removes All Traces from his Room

If the stuffed gray cat stares face down
into a crate forever from now on, he will not care.
Bury the cross-stitched alphabet,

the carved Russian wolf, the wooden train,
— where did all that come from anyway?
Even the pencilled height marks on the wall got

covered over by fresh paint — why keep them
when he doesn't like the lost kid with long hair anyway,
who cares how tall he wasn't?

The palette shrinks: black, white, gray.
Somewhere he saw an image of a monk's cell,
spartan clean. He will make a box for his shoes.

Wires tangle behind a desk.
Adaptors, surge protectors — defend us all.
At night he hears a weird clacking in the leaves

that might be an animal and the late train wailing
on its long way west. *Why does it make so much noise?*
Doesn't it want to go?

Rico's Dog

Well, when Rico died, his dog did not die, that was the problem. The creamy-brown roundness of dog, some waddling spaniel mix with extra pounds around the middle, Rico's partner in walking and sitting, was suddenly bereft. As was Rico's wife, who told me never to thank anyone for a plant gift or it would wilt, and their kind grown daughter, both of whom lived with him in the steep blue-and-white house with an upper-story porch he added himself. And all the houses a hundred years old and the neighbors who had grown so used to Rico crossing the street with his dog, holding court in the wide green park, under the arching pecan trees. Rico was watching. That was one thing we could count on. Like heat in summer and the street lamp with a short in its wires kicking on and off. He was staring into the air, taking note of the old blocks with their predictable bends and curbs, the open-air trolleys rumbling past, the buses and cars speeding up Main in the mornings or rolling back south in the afternoons. He was noting who drove too fast, who needed a new muffler, who was leaving a house earlier than usual. He raised one hand if he saw you seeing him, a funny little punch. Once he got miffed with me for pretending to speak Spanish better than I really do. Rico saw through. He saw the FOR LEASE sign go up on the abandoned candy factory and knew no one would lease that place for years. He smiled. His dog circled the concrete bench a few times before sprawling at Rico's feet. Rico leaned forward to place his hand firmly on its blonde back. Something we could count. One man, one dog. We knew he drank from a bottle in a sack but don't we all, in our own ways? Rico leaned on his front gate when he wasn't in the park. He fixed plumbing if you begged him to. He scrubbed the head of the concrete cherub in the birdbath when his wife pointed it out. But his shocking departure, in the middle of a bright day, punching his fist to no one, was a jolt we could not have predicted. Tell you how lonesome a neighborhood can feel? Even when it has said goodbye to so many? A different thing to lose the watcher. A different kind of light without him in it. A different hum in the air with one dog walking in circles on the porch, inside the gate, and looking, looking, for Rico.

Interview, Saudi Arabia

The fathers do not know *— TYPICAL2 BLAME PARENTS, BURDEN OF FATHER.*
what the sons have done.
They are waiting for the sons to call home,
to say it was a mistake,
it was not me. — ITALIZED FOR EMPHASIS   X EMISKBMENT
Somewhere on another street
their boys in short white pants
are walking proudly
in a world they love.
Oranges peeled by hand,
frying onions,
marbles in dust. — DUE TO BLASTING
Whatever might happen
is shiny, strong.

One of the sons was sad sometimes. — SIGNS OF DEPRESSION
No one knew why.
There is *no way*, says his brother,
he could fly a plane. — AGAIN ITALIZED EMPHASIS

The fathers blink back tears. → ALLITERATION OF SIMILAR SOUNDING WORDS.
They have no evidence at all.
Please tell them something better.
Their sons went to school,
were normal, good.
Whatever would happen
might still be changed.

It is not a game, it was never a game.

It was a girl's arm, the right one
that held a pencil.
She liked her arm.

It was a small stone house
with an iron terrace,
a flower pot beside the
door.

People passing,
loaves of bread,
little plans
the size of a thought,
dropping off something you borrowed,
buying a small sack of *zaater*,
it was a hand with fingers
dipping the scoop into the barrel.

I will not live this way,
said a woman with a baby on her hip
but she was where she was.

These men do not represent me,
said the teacher with her students
in pressed blue smocks.

They had sharpened their pencils.
Desks lined in a simple room.
It was school,
numbers on a page.
a radiant sky with clouds.
In the old days you felt happy to see it.

No one wanted anything
to drop out of it
except rain. Where was rain?

It was not a game, it was
unbelievable sorrow
and fear.

A hand that a mother held.
A pocket. A glass.
It was not war.
It was people.

We had gone nowhere
in a million years.

The Light that Shines on Us Now

This strange beam of being right,
smug spotlight.
What else could we have done?
asks a little one.
What else?

Three girls with book bags
fleeing tanks.

Now that we are so bold,
now that we pretend
God likes some kinds of killing,
how will we deserve
the light of candles,
soft beam of a small lamp
falling across any safe bed?

Orphan boy in a striped shirt
trapped between two glum uncles.
He carries his mother's
smooth fragrance
and father's solid voice.
They were not countries,
they were continents.

Johnny Carson in Baghdad

What if we had sent Johnny to Baghdad
instead of all those other folks,
all that hardened apparatus,
all those dun-colored supplies?

It would have cost less, even if we paid him
what he was worth. Maybe we could have sent
a curtain with him, so he could walk out everywhere,
surprising people with his endless cheer,

lifting his eyebrows when someone said something
weird, handing Saddam a monkey, or a tarantula,
at an appropriate moment, asking the right questions
that would make things fall into focus,

inspiring the vast Middle Eastern laugh
so buried in these times.
Who do you trust?
He might have put on that turban too,

or dressed as a woman now and then,
and things would have gone better.
If they got rough he could invite the little bear
to drink out of someone's coffee cup

and I promise, no one would have harmed him,
or wanted to.
He would never have broken down a door
or been cruel to a prisoner,

but when everyone was laughing, might have done
some sleight-of-hand to move people

to a better place, make them look
agreeable, more agreeable, more *like* one another,

the way they truly are, instead of this stupid
wreckage that lessens us
on both sides of the sea.
Don't you wish?

I Feel Sorry for Jesus

People won't leave Him alone.
I know He said, *wherever two or more
are gathered in my name . . .*
but I'll bet some days He regrets it.

Cozily they tell you what He wants
and doesn't want
as if they just got an e-mail.
Remember "Telephone," that pass-it-on game

where the message changed dramatically
by the time it rounded the circle?
Well.
People blame terrible pieties on Jesus.

They want to be his special pet.
Jesus deserves better.
I think He's been exhausted
for a very long time.

He went *into the desert*, friends.
He didn't go into the pomp.
He didn't go into
the golden chandeliers

and say, *the truth tastes better here.*
See? I'm talking like I know.
It's dangerous talking for Jesus.
You get carried away almost immediately.

I stood in the spot where He was born.
I closed my eyes where He died and didn't die.

Every twist of the Via Dolorosa
was written on my skin.

And that makes me feel like being silent
for Him, you know? A secret pouch
of listening. You won't hear me
mention this again.

Mamma is Still About the Same

Well no she isn't, you know. Ever the same, minute to minute. She just seems that way to those who aren't inside that big dress. She's up and down. She's spun of fine wool, and twisted. Better some days, but rarely. She does not like being the Mamma all the time. Bring me that cool rag, you hear? Bring me a bite of lemon sponge. Bring me something from school that has an A on it for a change. No, she doesn't want to cross the river ever again, after the flood. Even though the water went down, she has a bad feeling about it. She got that knot on her head. No one can figure it out or take it off.

Working on his Sermon

He always said *Shhhhhhhhh*
to keep us out of the room.
Herding the children into the hall,
beyond the shut door or the door ajar
on his cluttered study,
lamp casting a soft yellow funnel
over the desk,
and we were not invited in,
to spin our words or blue-eyed marbles
on the floor, to help him see
the grit of religion
come to life.

A stern man, handsome
in photographs but disinclined
to emotion, he forbade us to grieve
at his wife's funeral, our poor grandmother,
Shhhhhhh, if I find you crying,
you will be in trouble with me.

But we were already in trouble,
being already born, born to a sadness
larger than one family,
one straight-talking no-nonsense family,
a legacy of secret tears, silence,
keeping it in and keeping it out.
Shhhhhhhh, he was working on a
paragraph, a closing, he was trying out
forgiveness, slipping his hand
into the coarse sleeve of sympathy,
grappling with the other cheek.
And the congregation was critical, bickering

behind his back, sending a stream of letters,
wishing he had said it differently,
said it only in German,
why didn't he like their clubs and sociability?
And every single week
had a sermon in it, for years and years.
It was hard to be so earnest and grim in any language,
to do the Lord's work so long before
going into hiding, closing the shades,
sending his son Theo to the pulpit in his place.

Music

When you wanted a piano
everyone wanted something:
your sister wished for a red silk dress
with polka-dots,
your mother, a gold watch
to hold the time
that kept leaving her
before she could find it.
Even your father,
who spent hours calculating
figures in a checkbook,
wanted a green car
with fancy headlights,
a venetian blind
that didn't stick.

That was the first lesson.

You made a paper keyboard
and played it in the dark,
singing the notes.
If you pressed your foot
you could feel a pedal in the carpet,
hear the murmur lasting beyond itself
the way it did when they played
piano at school.
Everyone would leave the music class
while you stood hinged to that last tone
emptying into air. It wasn't gone
if you tilted your head.

Your father found the keyboard
and slapped you for wasting paper.

The second lesson was long.

❖

My Perfect Stranger

The little girl at the airport gate in Cincinnati had a tuft of vivid pink ponytail sticking straight up out of her brown-haired head. I wondered how hard she had to beg to get her mother to do that. She was about five, wearing a lacy white party dress. When we boarded the plane she turned up sitting right in front of me. She poked her cute little face through the crack between the seats. "Do *you* have a table that comes out of your arm?" "Say what?" She had the bulkhead seat, with an armrest that opened for the hidden tray to pop out. "No," I laughed. "I just have a regular table that folds down." "Oh, too bad." When the flight attendant gave safety instructions over the loudspeaker, the girl chimed out loud responses. "You're welcome!" to "Thanks for flying with us." "Hope you have a nice flight too!" Her mother tried to shush her. "But you told me to answer people," the girl protested. The mama said, "That lady's talking to everyone. She's not just talking to you." The plane took off toward San Francisco and the little girl looked down on Cincinnati. "Oh Mama!" she cried. "We forget we live in a zigzag world. Look how it's shining!" Tears filled my eyes. Sometimes, if you're lucky, you get to fly behind a poet. The girl turned the pages of exotic merchandise in the airport catalog. "Mama, someday if we're rich, can we buy all this?" Oh honey, I thought, you're rich right now. She stuck her face through the crack again. "Find me!" she ordered. Meaning, which side of the seat will I peek around next? Then she stared at me very hard. "I think you need a picture. You look tired. Could I draw you one? What do you want? You look like you need a tree." But she drew a blue flower with green leaves, tall as the person next to it, who happened to be wearing glasses like mine. Then she asked how to spell my name and wrote TO NAOMI, LOVE

LAYLA across the top. Oh Layla . . . I wanted to whisper to her that we shared more than a flight. The familiar accent of the Middle East flavored her mother's voice. When I was little, I wished my name were Layla too. But what would have happened had I announced our ethnic link to such an outspoken little artist? Her voice, like a flute, might have exclaimed it, "We're Arabs!" and we were on a plane. I didn't mention it. But Layla, you charmed me. (By the way, I kept your flower.)

I Never Realized They Had Aspirations Like Ours

An Israeli, about the Palestinians

Cranes which land in a Texas river
have flown for thousands of miles.
Dipping long beaks into green water,
they pretend not to notice us.
Graceful necks,
a curved, close world.
Still, a feather fluffs
or a wing stays wide
if we pass.

What else but the long stroke of hope?
Some have said it fifty years.
By now the sorrowing people
make secret refuge in the sky.
If the ground satisfied their dreams,
the sky would miss them.

Truth Serum

We made it from the ground-up corn in the old back
    pasture.
Pinched a scent of night jasmine billowing off the fence,
popped it right in.
That frog song wanting nothing but echo?
We used that.
Stirred it widely. Noticed the clouds while stirring.
Called upon our ancient great aunts and their long slow eyes
of summer. Dropped in their names.
Added a mint leaf now and then
to hearten the broth. Added a note of cheer and worry.
Orange butterfly between the claps of thunder?
Perfect. And once we had it,
had smelled and tasted the fragrant syrup,
placing the pan on a back burner for keeping,
the sorrow lifted in small ways.
We boiled down the lies in another pan till they
    disappeared.
We washed that pan.

ABOUT THE AUTHOR

Naomi Shihab Nye lives in San Antonio, Texas. Her books include *A Maze Me: Poems for Girls*; *Going Going* (a novel for teens); *19 Varieties of Gazelle*; *Poems of the Middle East* (a National Book Award finalist); *Come with Me: Poems for a Journey*; *Baby Radar*; *Sitti's Secrets*; *Red Suitcase* and *Habibi*, a novel for teens which won six Best Book awards and was turned into a play on stage, adapted by Paul Bonin-Rodriguez. She has edited seven anthologies of poetry for young readers, including *This Same Sky*; *The Tree is Older than You Are*; *The Space Between our Footsteps: Poems & Paintings from the Middle East*; *What Have You Lost?*; *Salting the Ocean* and *Is This Forever or What? Poems and Paintings from Texas*. A visiting writer for many years all over the world, she has been a Lannan Foundation Fellow, a Guggenheim Fellow and a Library of Congress Witter Bynner Fellow.

ACKNOWLEDGMENTS

Grateful acknowledgment is made to the editors of the
following journals and books, in which some of these poems
first appeared: *Borderlands, Cider Press Review, New
Letters, Double Room: A Journal of Prose Poetry & Flash
Fiction, One Trick Pony, Water-Stone Review, Spiritus,
Redactions, Organica, Christian Century, Poetry 180,*
edited by Billy Collins, and a chapbook, *Cross that Line*
(Lost Canyon, Baksdale, Texas).

Many thanks to Patrick Lannan and the Lannan
Foundation, the Lannan Writers Residency in Marfa, Texas,
and Steven, Kathryn and Sara at the Steven Barclay Agency,
and Thom Ward, my editor at BOA Editions, Ltd.

BOA EDITIONS, LTD.
AMERICAN POETS CONTINUUM SERIES

No. 1   *The Fuhrer Bunker:*
        A Cycle of Poems in
        Progress
        W. D. Snodgrass

No. 2   *She*
        M. L. Rosenthal

No. 3   *Living With Distance*
        Ralph J. Mills, Jr.

No. 4   *Not Just Any Death*
        Michael Waters

No. 5   *That Was Then:*
        New and Selected Poems
        Isabella Gardner

No. 6   *Things That Happen*
        Where There Aren't Any
        People
        William Stafford

No. 7   *The Bridge of Change:*
        Poems 1974–1980
        John Logan

No. 8   *Signatures*
        Joseph Stroud

No. 9   *People Live Here:*
        Selected Poems
        1949–1983
        Louis Simpson

No. 10 *Yin*
        Carolyn Kizer

No. 11 *Duhamel: Ideas of Order*
        in Little Canada
        Bill Tremblay

No. 12 *Seeing It Was So*
        Anthony Piccione

No. 13 *Hyam Plutzik:*
        The Collected Poems

No. 14 *Good Woman: Poems*
        and
        a Memoir 1969–1980
        Lucille Clifton

No. 15 *Next: New Poems*
        Lucille Clifton

No. 16 *Roxa: Voices of the*
        Culver Family
        William B. Patrick

No. 17 *John Logan:*
        The Collected Poems

No. 18 *Isabella Gardner:*
        The Collected Poems

No. 19 *The Sunken Lightship*
        Peter Makuck

No. 20 *The City in Which I Love*
        You
        Li-Young Lee

No. 21 *Quilting: Poems*
        1987–1990
        Lucille Clifton

No. 22 *John Logan:*
        The Collected Fiction

No. 23 *Shenandoah and Other*
        Verse Plays
        Delmore Schwartz

No. 24 *Nobody Lives on*
        Arthur Godfrey
        Boulevard
        Gerald Costanzo

No. 25 *The Book of Names:*
        New and Selected Poems
        Barton Sutter

No. 26 *Each in His Season*
        W. D. Snodgrass

No. 27 *Wordworks:*
        Poems Selected and New
        Richard Kostelanetz

No. 28 *What We Carry*
        Dorianne Laux

No. 29 *Red Suitcase*
        Naomi Shihab Nye

No. 30 *Song*
        Brigit Pegeen Kelly

No. 31 *The Fuehrer Bunker:*
        The Complete Cycle
        W. D. Snodgrass

COLOPHON

The Isabella Gardner Poetry Award is given biennially to a poet in mid-career with a new book of exceptional merit. Poet, actress, and associate editor of *Poetry* magazine, Isabella Gardner (1915–1981) published five celebrated collections of poetry, was three times nominated for the National Book Award, and was the first recipient of the New York State Walt Whitman Citation of Merit for Poetry. She championed the work of young and gifted poets, helping many of them to find publication.

You & Yours by Naomi Shihab Nye was set in Sabon by Scott McCarney, Rochester, New York. The cover design was by Geri McCormick. The cover art, "Buzzload of Paranoia" by Charles Moody, is courtesy of the artist. Manufacturing by McNaughton & Gunn, Ann Arbor, Michigan.

The publication of this book was made possible, in part, by the special support of the following individuals:

Nelson Adrian Blish
Alan & Nancy Cameros
Gwen & Gary Conners
Burch & Louise Craig
Bradley P. & Debra
    Kang Dean
Suzanne & Peter Durant
Richard & Suressa Forbes
Dr. Henry & Beverly French
Marla Friedrich
Andy & Jacquie Germanow
Dane & Judy Gordon
Emil Gottwald
Donald & Marjorie Grinols
Kip & Deb Hale
Noël Hanlon &
    Peter Koehler, Jr.
Kit Abel Hawkins
Peter & Robin Hursh
Robert & Willy Hursh
Frank W. Jennings

X.J. Kennedy
Louise H. Klinke
Laurie Kutchins
Archie & Pat Kutz
Rosemary & Lewis Lloyd
Barbara & John Lovenheim
John & Billie Maguire
Robert & Francie Marx
Desmond H. Murphy
Boo Poulin
Deborah Ronnen
Paul & Andrea Rubery
Paul Tortorella
Harry P. & Karen E. Trueheart
George & Bonnie Wallace
Thomas R. Ward
Michael Waters
Glenn & Helen William
Stephen Wilson
Pat & Michael Wilder